BUILDING BLOCKS OF BIOLOGY

DRUGS AND VACCINES

Written by Alex Woolf

Illustrated by Ruth Bennett

www.worldbook.com

Co-published by agreement between Shi Tu Hui and World Book, Inc.

Shi Tu Hui
Room 1807, Block 1,
#3 West Dawang Road
Chaoyang District, Beijing 100025
P.R. China

World Book, Inc.
180 North LaSalle Street
Suite 900
Chicago, Illinois 60601
USA

© 2026. All rights reserved. This volume may not be reproduced in whole or in part in any form without prior written permission from the publisher.

WORLD BOOK and the GLOBE DEVICE are registered trademarks or trademarks of World Book, Inc.

Library of Congress Control Number: 2025942743

Building Blocks of Biology
ISBN: 978-0-7166-6737-7 (set, hard cover)

Drugs and Vaccines
ISBN: 978-0-7166-6746-9 (hard cover)

Also available as:
ISBN: 978-0-7166-6766-7 (e-book)
ISBN: 978-0-7166-6756-8 (soft cover)

WORLD BOOK STAFF

Editorial

Vice President
Tom Evans

Senior Manager, New Content
Jeff De La Rosa

Proofreader
Nathalie Strassheim

Graphics and Design

Senior Visual Communications Designer
Melanie Bender

Acknowledgments
Writer: Alex Woolf
Illustrator: Ruth Bennett/The Bright Agency

TABLE OF CONTENTS

Disease 4

Drugs 8

Prescriptions 12

Dangers of Drugs 16

Science Fun with Fur:
Medicine Safety Challenge 18

Antibiotics 20

Immune System 26

Vaccines 30

Life on the Edge: AI-Assisted Drug Discovery ... 34

Show What You Know 38

Answers and Words to Know 40

There is a glossary on page 40. Terms defined in the glossary are in type **that looks like this** on their first appearance.

A drug is a chemical that has an effect on the body...

A drug you take when you don't feel well is called medicine...

Medicine can make you feel better.

SCIENCE FUN WITH FUR!

MEDICINE SAFETY CHALLENGE

How much do you know about medicine safety? Take this quiz to find out!

TRUE OR FALSE

① My friend used this medicine last week for his sore throat. It worked for him. There's still some left. I should take some for *my* sore throat.

② Medicines should be kept out of the reach of children.

③ It is important to take the amount stated on the bottle or packet.

④ If someone is ill, any medicine will help them.

⑤ Always read the instructions before taking medicine.

⑥ Children can give themselves medication if they are old enough to read the label.

⑦ Medicines last forever.

See page 40 for answers.

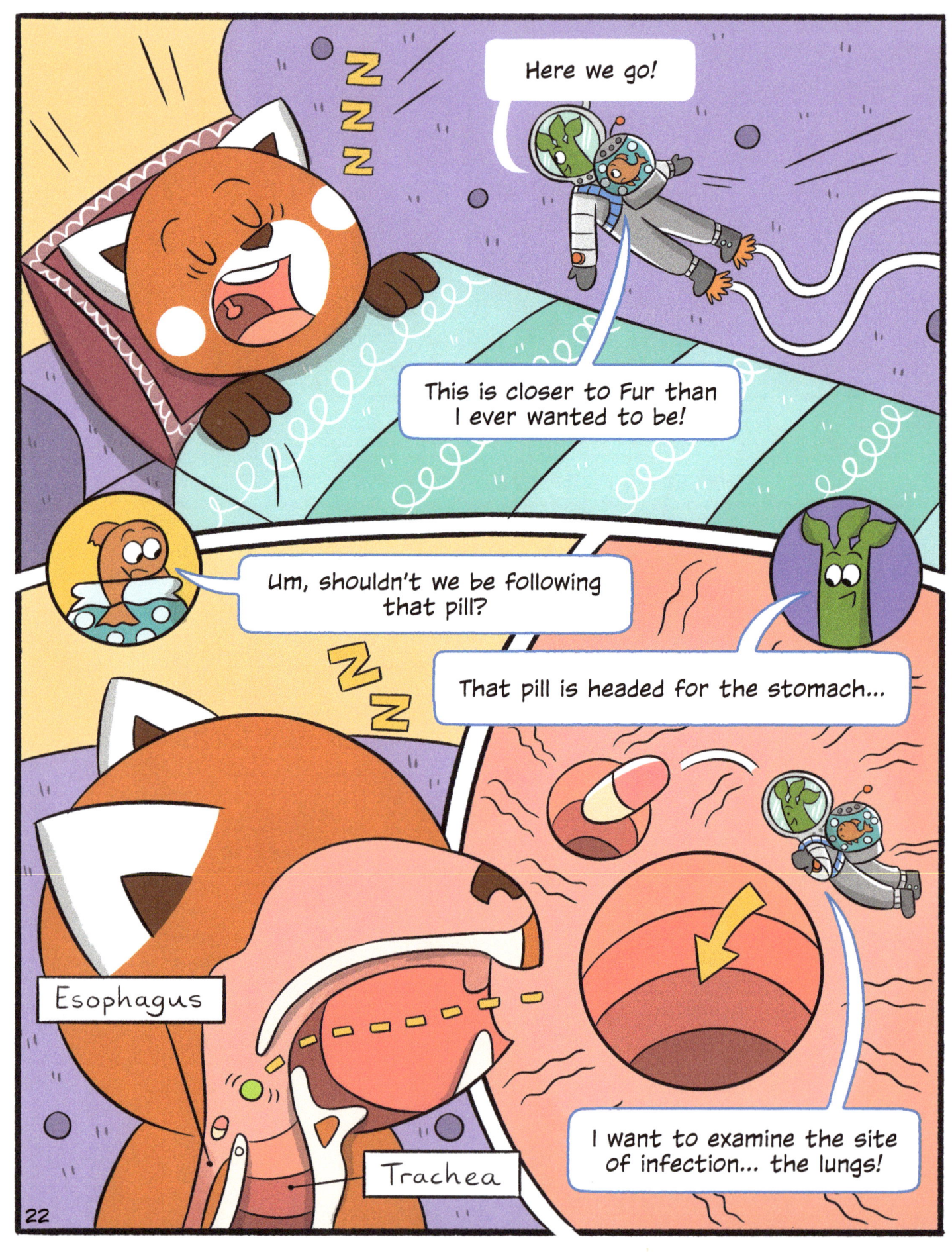

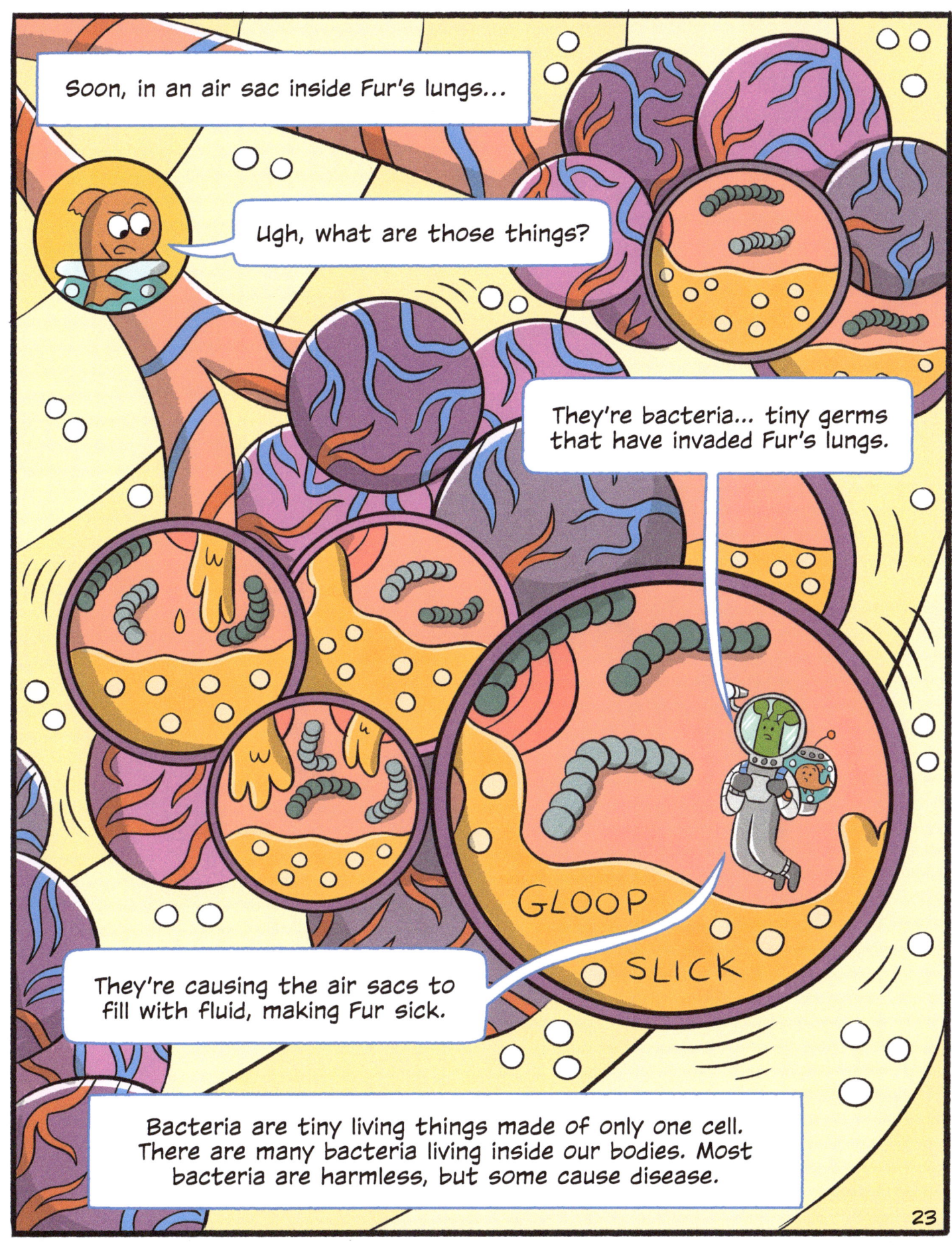

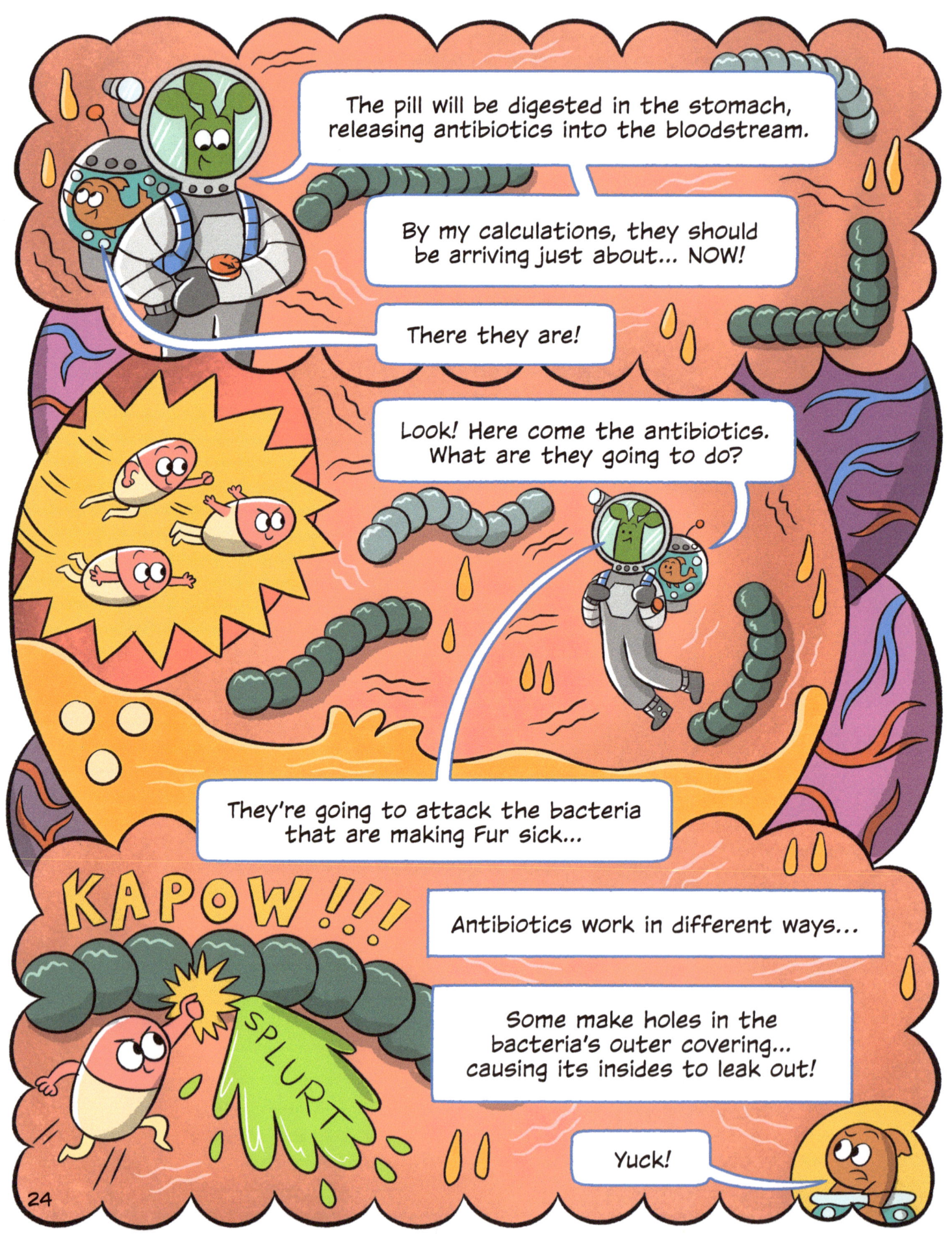

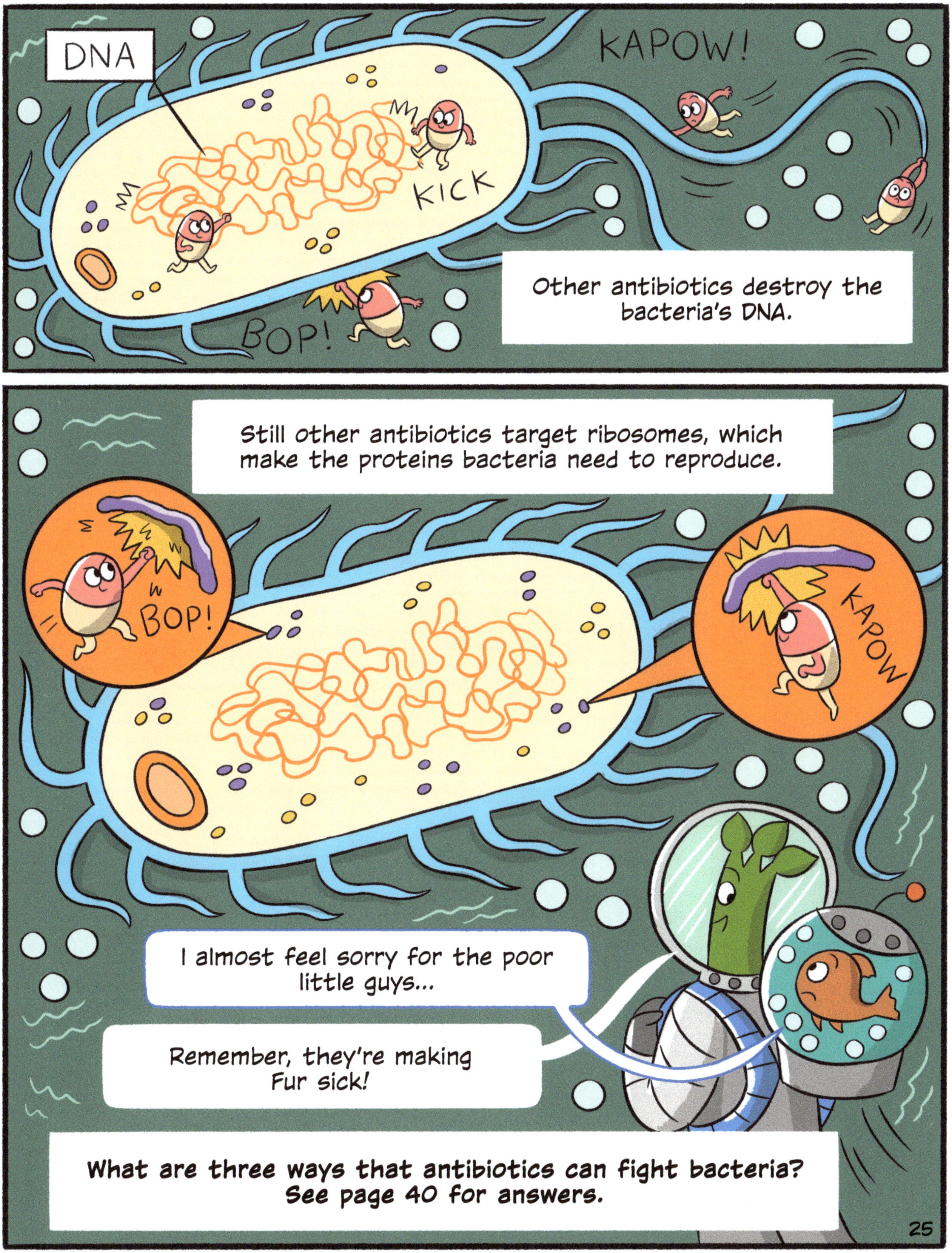

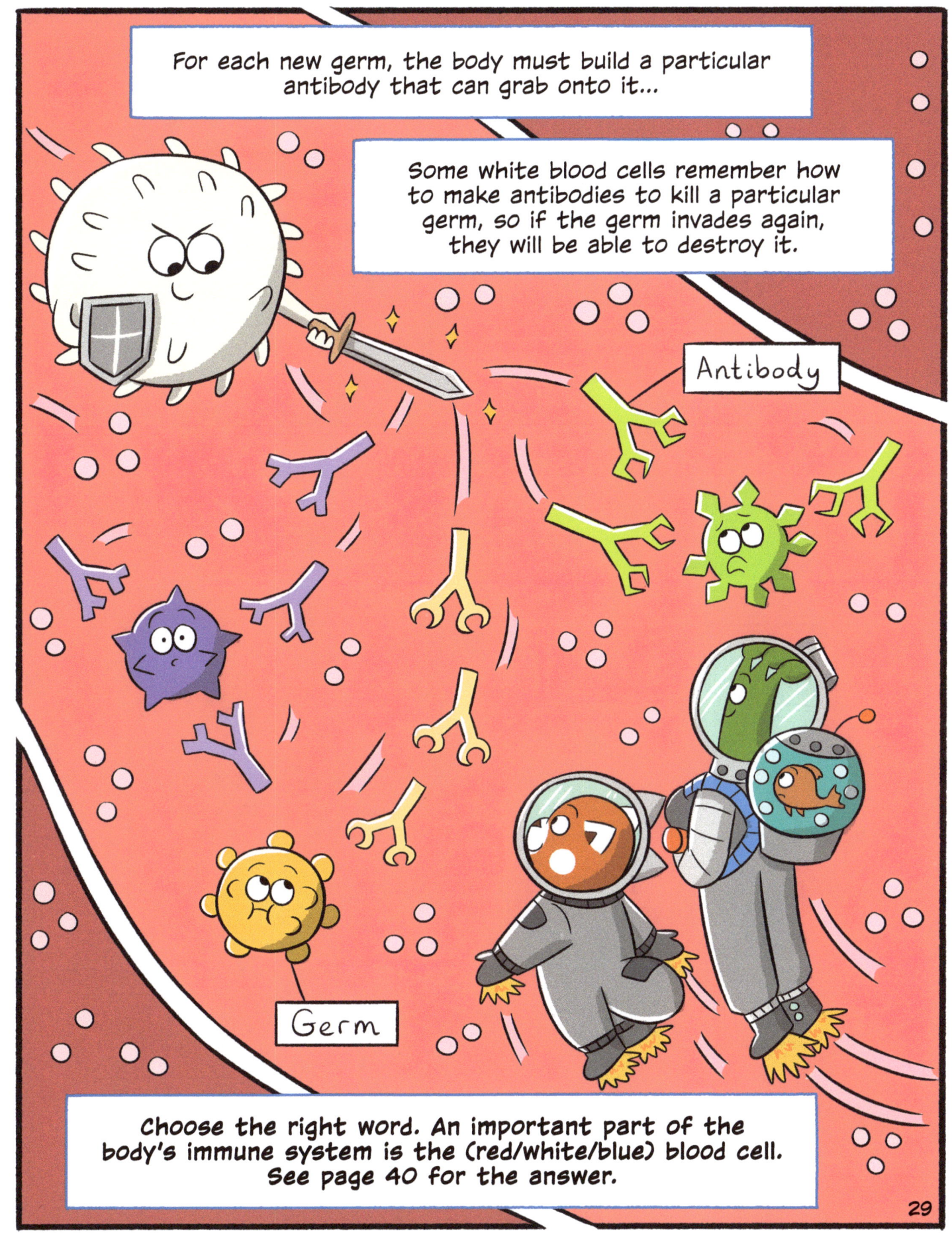

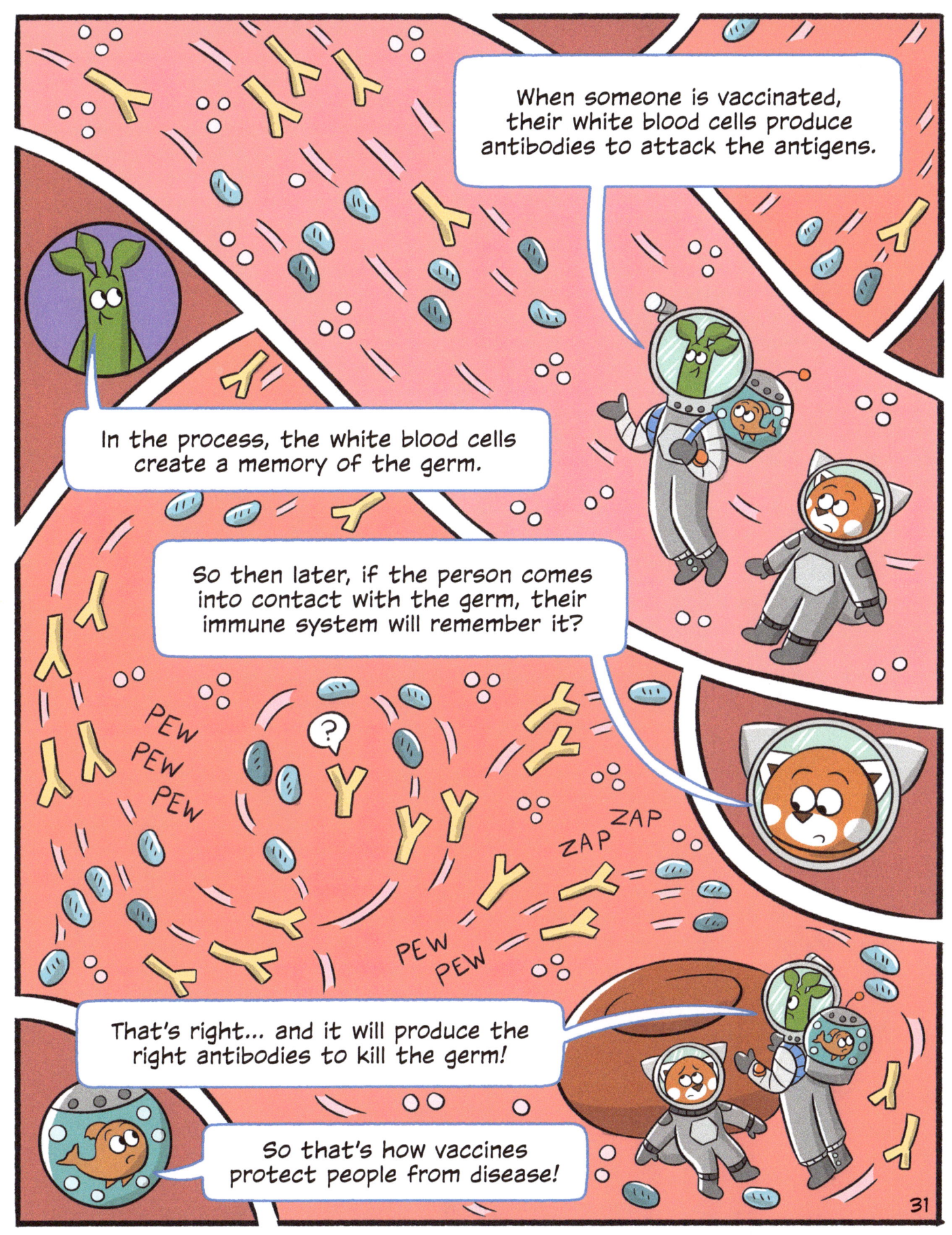

"The vaccine taught your white blood cells how to fight off the flu germs, Grandma!"

"We know because we saw them doing it..."

"You are funny, Fin! How could you possibly have seen that?"

The next day...

"I'm so glad you're feeling better for your birthday, Fur!"

"Me, too. It's no fun being sick."

"Luckily, we have medicines that can make us better..."

"And cake... Cake cures everything!"

SHOW WHAT YOU KNOW

1. How many types of factors that can cause disease can you name?

2. Match each word to its definition.

disease
drug
prescription
symptom

A. a chemical that has an effect on the body
B. a sign of illness
C. a disorder of the body or mind
D. a doctor's order for a particular medicine

3. Fill in the blanks.

A. A medicine called an _____ can be used to fight a bacterial infection.
B. The body's _____ system works to fight of illness. Much of this work is done by _____ blood cells.

4. Choose the right word.

A. An (antibiotic/vaccine) works by teaching the immune system to fight off illness.
B. The immune system manufactures chemicals called (antigens/antibodies) to fight off germs. These latch on to parts of the germs called (antigens/antibodies).

See page 40 for answers.

ANSWERS

page 9: body; mind

page 11: symptoms

page 15: prescription

pages 18 and 19: 1. False; 2. True; 3. True; 4. False; 5. True; 6. False; 7. False

page 25: Antibiotics can fight bacteria by breaking holes in their outer coating, destroying their DNA, or targeting ribosomes, which make proteins bacteria need to reproduce.

page 29: white

SHOW WHAT YOU KNOW ANSWERS
pages 38-39:

1. Types of factors that can cause disease include harmful germs, allergic reactions, lifestyle factors, and inheritance (see pages 6 and 7).

2. A. drug
   B. symptom
   C. disease
   D. prescription

3. A. antibiotic
   B. immune; white

4. A. vaccine
   B. antibodies; antigens

WORDS TO KNOW

antibiotic a medicine used to fight bacterial infection.

antibodies proteins manufactured by the immune system that attach to and destroy germs.

antigen part of a germ to which an antibody can attach.

disease a disorder of the body or mind.

drug a chemical that has an effect on the body.

immune system the system of the body involved in fighting disease.

pharmacy a place where prescriptions are used to obtain drugs.

prescription a written order by a doctor for a particular drug or treatment.

side effect an unintended effect that a medicine may have on the body.

symptom a sign of an illness.

vaccine a medicine that "teaches" the body's immune system how to fight a particular illness.

www.ingramcontent.com/pod-product-compliance
Lightning Source LLC
Chambersburg PA
CBHW061256170426
43191CB00041B/2434